学校 - school 2
旅行 - travel 5
輸送 - transport 8
都市 - city 10
風景 - landscape 14
レストラン - restaurant 17
スーパーマーケット - supermarket 20
飲み物 - drinks 22
食べ物 - food 23
農場 - farm 27
家 - house 31
リビングルーム - living room 33
台所 - kitchen 35
浴室 - bathroom 38
子供部屋 - child's room 42
衣服 - clothing 44
オフィス - office 49
経済 - economy 51
職業 - occupations 53
道具 - tools 56
楽器 - musical instruments 57
動物園 - zoo 59
スポーツ - sports 62
活動 - activities 63
家族 - family 67
体 - body 68
病院 - hospital 72
救急 - emergency 76
地球 - Earth 77
時計 - clock 79
週 - week 80
年 - year 81
形 - shapes 83
色 - colours 84
反対 - opposites 85
数 - numbers 88
言語 - languages 90
誰 / 何 / どう - who / what / how 91
どこ - where 92

Impressum
Verlag: BABADADA GmbH, Nedderfeld 112 , 22529 Hamburg
Geschäftsführer / Verlagsleitung: Harald Hof
Druck: Books on Demand GmbH, In de Tarpen 42, 22848 Norderstedt

Imprint
Publisher: BABADADA GmbH, Nedderfeld 112 , 22529 Hamburg, Germany
Managing Director / Publishing direction: Harald Hof
Print: Books on Demand GmbH, In de Tarpen 42, 22848 Norderstedt

学校
school

割り算
divide

186/2

黒板
board

教室
classroom

校庭
school yard

教師
teacher

紙
paper

ペン
pen

書く
write

事務机
desk

定規
ruler

本
book

生徒
pupil

ランドセル

satchel

筆入れ

pencil case

鉛筆

pencil

鉛筆削り

pencil sharpener

消しゴム

rubber

スケッチブック

drawing pad

スケッチ
drawing

絵筆
paintbrush

絵の具箱
paint box

はさみ
scissors

接着剤
glue

練習帳
exercise book

宿題
homework

12

数
number

2+2

足し算
add

5-2

引き算
subtract

2×2

かけ算
multiply

計算する
calculate

A

文字
letter

ABCDEFG
HIJKLMN
OPQRSTU
VWXYZ

アルファベット
alphabet

hello

単語
word

テキスト

text

読む

read

チョーク

chalk

授業

lesson

学級日誌

register

試験

exam

通知表

certificate

制服

school uniform

教育

education

百科事典

encyclopedia

大学

university

顕微鏡

microscope

地図

map

ごみ箱

waste-paper basket

ホテル
hotel

ホステル
hostel

両替所
bureau de change

スーツケース
suitcase

自動車
car

言語
language

はい / いいえ
yes / no

問題ない
Okay

ハロー
hello

翻訳者
translator

ありがとう
Thank you

…はいくらですか？

how much is…?

わかりません

I do not understand

問題

problem

こんばんは！

Good evening!

おはようございます！

Good morning!

おやすみなさい！

Good night!

さようなら

bye bye

方向

direction

手荷物

luggage

バッグ

bag

リュックサック

backpack

お客様

guest

部屋

room

寝袋

sleeping bag

テント

tent

旅行者情報
tourist information

ビーチ
beach

クレジットカード
credit card

朝食
breakfast

昼食
lunch

夕食
dinner

チケット
ticket

エレベーター
lift

スタンプ
stamp

境界
border

税関
customs

大使館
embassy

ビザ
visa

パスポート
passport

輸送

transport

飛行機
aeroplane

船
ship

消防車
fire engine

バス
bus

トラック
truck

モーターボート
motorboat

自動車
car

自転車
bike

フェリー

ferry

ボート

boat

バイク

motorbike

パトカー

police car

レーシングカー

racing car

レンタカー

rental car

カーシェアリング
car sharing

レッカー車
breakdown truck

ごみ収集車
refuse truck

モーター
motor

燃料
fuel

ガソリンスタンド
petrol station

交通標識
traffic sign

交通
traffic

渋滞
traffic jam

駐車場
car park

駅
train station

道
tracks

列車
train

路面電車
tram

車両
carriage

ヘリコプター

helicopter

空港

airport

タワー

tower

乗客

passenger

コンテナ

container

段ボール箱

carton

カート

cart

カゴ

basket

離陸 / 着陸

take off / land

都市

city

村

village

都心

city centre

家

house

映画館
cinema

宣伝
advert

街灯
street lamp

CINEMA

通り
street

タクシー
taxi

キオスク
snack shop

歩行者
pedestrian

舗道
pavement

横断歩道
zebra crossing

ゴミ箱
bin

交差点
crossing

信号
traffic lights

小屋
hut

アパート
flat

駅
train station

市役所
town hall

美術館
museum

学校
school

都市 - city

大学

university

銀行

bank

病院

hospital

ホテル

hotel

薬局

pharmacy

オフィス

office

書店

book shop

ショップ

shop

花屋

florist's

スーパーマーケット

supermarket

市場

market

デパート

department store

魚屋

fishmonger's

ショッピングセンター

shopping centre

港

harbour

公園
park

ベンチ
bench

橋
bridge

階段
stairs

地下鉄
underground

トンネル
tunnel

バス停
bus stop

バー
bar

レストラン
restaurant

ポスト
postbox

道路標識
street sign

パーキングメーター
parking meter

動物園
zoo

スイミングプール
swimming pool

モスク
mosque

農場

farm

汚染

pollution

墓地

graveyard

教会

church

遊び場

playground

寺

temple

風景

landscape

葉
leaf

道標
signpost

道
way

草地
meadow

石
stone

木
tree

ハイカー
hiker

川
river

草
grass

花
flower

谷
valley

山
hill

湖
lake

森
forest

砂漠
desert

火山
volcano

城
castle

虹
rainbow

キノコ
mushroom

ヤシの木
palm tree

蚊
mosquito

ハエ
fly

蟻
ant

ミツバチ
bee

クモ
spider

カブトムシ

beetle

蛙

frog

リス

squirrel

ハリネズミ

hedgehog

ウサギ

hare

フクロウ

owl

鳥

bird

白鳥

swan

雄豚

boar

鹿

deer

ヘラジカ

moose

ダム

dam

風力タービン

wind turbine

ソーラーパネル

solar panel

気候

climate

ウェイター
waiter

メニュー
menu

椅子
chair

スープ
soup

ピザ
pizza

刃物類
cutlery

テーブルクロス
tablecloth

前菜
starter

メインコース
main course

デザート
dessert

飲み物
drinks

食べ物
food

ボトル
bottle

ファストフード

fast food

屋台の食べ物

street food

ティーポット

teapot

砂糖入れ

sugar bowl

一人前

portion

エスプレッソマシン

espresso machine

幼児用食事椅子

high chair

請求書

bill

トレー

tray

ナイフ

knife

フォーク

fork

スプーン

spoon

ティースプーン

teaspoon

ナプキン

serviette

グラス

glass

皿

plate

スープ皿

soup plate

受け皿

saucer

ソース

sauce

塩入れ

salt pot

ペッパーミル

pepper mill

酢

vinegar

油

oil

スパイス

spices

ケチャップ

ketchup

マスタード

mustard

マヨネーズ

mayonnaise

スーパーマーケット
supermarket

特価品
special offer

顧客
customer

乳製品
dairy

果物
fruit

ショッピング
・カート
trolley

肉屋
butcher's

パン屋
baker's

重さをはかる
weigh

野菜
vegetables

肉
meat

冷凍食品
frozen food

冷肉の薄切り

cold meat

缶詰食品

tinned food

洗剤

washing powder

菓子

sweets

家庭用品

household products

清掃用品

cleaning products

販売員

salesperson

現金箱

till

レジ係

cashier

買い物リスト

shopping list

開館時刻

opening hours

財布

wallet

クレジットカード

credit card

バッグ

bag

ポリ袋

plastic bag

水

water

ジュース

juice

牛乳

milk

コーラ

coke

ワイン

wine

ビール

beer

アルコール

alcohol

ココア

cocoa

紅茶

tea

コーヒー

coffee

エスプレッソ

espresso

カプチーノ

cappuccino

バナナ

banana

リンゴ

apple

オレンジ

orange

メロン

melon

レモン

lemon

ニンジン

carrot

ニンニク

garlic

竹

bamboo

玉ねぎ

onion

キノコ

mushroom

ナッツ

nuts

ヌードル

noodles

スパゲッティ

spaghetti

米

rice

サラダ

salad

フライドポテト

chips

フライドポテト

fried potatoes

ピザ

pizza

ハンバーガー

hamburger

サンドウィッチ

sandwich

カツレツ

cutlet

ハム

ham

サラミ

salami

ソーセージ

sausage

鶏肉

chicken

焼き

roast

魚

fish

麦のお粥

porridge oats

ムーズリ

muesli

コーンフレーク

cornflakes

小麦粉

flour

クロワッサン

croissant

ロールパン

bread roll

パン

bread

トースト

toast

ビスケット

biscuits

バター

butter

カッテージチーズ

curd

ケーキ

cake

卵

egg

目玉焼き

fried egg

チーズ

cheese

アイスクリーム

ice cream

砂糖

sugar

はちみつ

honey

ジャム

jam

ヌガークリーム

chocolate spread

カレー

curry

農家
farmhouse

納屋
barn

ストローベール
straw bale

畑
field

馬
horse

トレーラー
trailer

子馬
foal

トラクター
tractor

ロバ
donkey

子羊
lamb

羊
sheep

ヤギ
goat

雌牛
cow

子牛
calf

豚
pig

子豚
piglet

雄牛
bull

ガチョウ

goose

アヒル

duck

ひよこ

chick

にわとり

hen

おんどり

cock

ネズミ

rat

猫

cat

ねずみ

mouse

雄牛

ox

犬

dog

犬小屋

doghouse

散水ホース

garden hose

じょうろ

watering can

大鎌

scythe

すき

plough

草刈り鎌

sickle

くわ

hoe

堆肥用フォーク

pitchfork

斧

axe

手押し車

wheelbarrow

かいばおけ

trough

牛乳缶

milk can

袋

sack

フェンス

fence

畜舎

stable

温室

greenhouse

土壌

soil

種

seed

肥料

fertilizer

コンバイン

combine harvester

収穫する

harvest

収穫

harvest

ヤマイモ

yams

小麦

wheat

大豆

soy

じゃがいも

potato

トウモロコシ

corn

菜種

rapeseed

果樹

fruit tree

キャッサバ

cassava

穀物

cereals

煙突
chimney

屋根
roof

排水管
drainpipe

窓
window

車庫
garage

呼び鈴
doorbell

ドア
door

ゴミ箱
rubbish bin

郵便受け
letterbox

庭
garden

リビングルーム

living room

浴室

bathroom

台所

kitchen

寝室

bedroom

子供部屋

child's room

ダイニング・ルーム

dining room

床

floor

壁

wall

天井

ceiling

地下貯蔵庫

cellar

サウナ

sauna

バルコニー

balcony

テラス

terrace

プール

pool

芝刈り機

lawn mower

シーツ

sheet

ベッドカバー

bedspread

ベッド

bed

ほうき

broom

バケツ

bucket

スイッチ

switch

壁紙
▶ wallpaper

絵
picture

ランプ
lamp ◀

棚
shelf

食器棚
cupboard

暖炉
fireplace

テレビ
television

花
flower

クッション
cushion

ソファ
sofa

花瓶
vase

リモコン
remote control

カーペット
carpet

カーテン
curtain

テーブル
table

椅子
chair

ロッキングチェア
rocking chair

ひじ掛け椅子
armchair

本
book

毛布
blanket

飾り
decoration

たきぎ
firewood

映画
film

ステレオ
hi-fi equipment

鍵
key

新聞
newspaper

絵画
painting

ポスター
poster

ラジオ
radio

メモ帳
notepad

掃除機
hoover

サボテン
cactus

ろうそく
candle

冷蔵庫
fridge

電子レンジ
microwave oven

調理用はかり
kitchen scales

トースター
toaster

洗剤
detergent

冷凍室
freezer

オーブン
oven

ゴミ箱
rubbish bin

食器洗い機
dishwasher

こんろ
cooker

鍋
pot

鉄鍋
cast-iron pot

中華鍋/ カダイ鍋
wok / kadai

フライパン
pan

やかん
kettle

蒸し器

steamer

天板

baking tray

食器

crockery

マグカップ

mug

ボウル

bowl

箸

chopsticks

おたま

ladle

へら

spatula

泡立て器

whisk

こし器

strainer

ふるい

sieve

すりおろし器

grater

すり鉢

mortar

バーベキュー

barbecue

かまど

open fire

台所 - kitchen

まな板

chopping board

麺棒

rolling pin

栓抜き

corkscrew

缶

can

缶切り

can opener

鍋つかみ

pot holder

流し

sink

ブラシ

brush

スポンジ

sponge

ミキサー

blender

冷凍庫

deep freezer

哺乳瓶

baby bottle

蛇口

tap

ヒーター
heating

タオル
towel

シャワー
shower

泡風呂
bubble bath

シャワーカーテン
shower curtain

浴槽
bathtub

洗濯機
washing machine

グラス
glass

蛇口
tap

タイル
tiles

おまる
potty

流し
sink

トイレ
toilet

和式トイレ
squat toilet

ビデ
bidet

小便器
urinal

トイレットペーパー
toilet paper

トイレブラシ
toilet brush

歯ブラシ

toothbrush

歯みがき

toothpaste

デンタルフロス

dental floss

洗う

wash

シャワーヘッド

handheld shower

ハンドビデ

douche

洗面台

basin

ボディブラシ

back brush

石鹸

soap

シャワー用ジェル

shower gel

シャンプー

shampoo

浴用タオル

flannel

排水口

drain

クリーム

cream

消臭

deodorant

鏡

mirror

手鏡

hand mirror

かみそり

razor

シェービング・フォーム

shaving foam

アフターシェーブローショ
ン

aftershave

櫛

comb

ブラシ

brush

ドライヤー

hair dryer

ヘアスプレー

hairspray

化粧

makeup

口紅

lipstick

マニキュア

nail varnish

脱脂綿

cotton wool

爪切り

nail scissors

香水

perfume

洗面用具入れ

washbag

スツール

stool

体重計

weighing scale

バスローブ

bathrobe

ゴム手袋

rubber gloves

タンポン

tampon

生理用ナプキン

sanitary towel

ケミカルトイレ

chemical toilet

目覚まし時計
alarm clock

ぬいぐるみ
cuddly toy

おもちゃの
自動車
toy car

ドール・ハウス
doll's house

プレゼント
present

がらがら
rattle

風船

balloon

ベッド

bed

ベビーカー

pram

カードゲーム

deck of cards

ジグソーパズル

jigsaw

漫画

comic

レゴ

lego bricks

玩具ブロック

building blocks

アクションフィギュア

action figure

ロンパース

babygrow

フリスビー

frisbee

モバイル

mobile

ボードゲーム

board game

さいころ

dice

鉄道模型

model train set

おしゃぶり

dummy

パーティー

party

絵本

picture book

ボール

ball

人形

doll

遊ぶ

play

砂場

sandpit

ブランコ

swing

おもちゃ

toys

ゲーム機

video game console

三輪車

tricycle

テディベア

teddy bear

衣装ダンス

wardrobe

衣服

clothing

靴下

socks

ストッキング

stockings

タイツ

tights

スカーフ
scarf

雨傘
umbrella

Tシャツ
t-shirt

ベルト
belt

ブーツ
boots

スリッパ
slippers

スニーカー
trainers

サンダル
sandals

靴
shoes

ゴム長靴
rubber boots

パンツ
underpants

ブラ
bra

ベスト
vest

衣服 - clothing

ボディースーツ

body

ズボン

trousers

ジーンズ

jeans

スカート

skirt

ブラウス

blouse

シャツ

shirt

セーター

pullover

パーカー

hoodie

ブレザー

blazer

ジャケット

jacket

コート

coat

レインコート

raincoat

服装

costume

ドレス

dress

ウェディングドレス

wedding dress

スーツ

suit

ナイトガウン

nightgown

パジャマ

pyjamas

サリー

sari

ヘッドスカーフ

headscarf

ターバン

turban

ブルカ

burqa

カフタン

kaftan

アバヤ

abaya

水着

swimsuit

トランクス

trunks

半ズボン

shorts

スウェットスーツ

tracksuit

エプロン

apron

手袋

gloves

ボタン

button

メガネ

glasses

ブレスレット

bracelet

ネックレス

necklace

指輪

ring

イヤリング

earring

帽子

cap

ハンガー

coat hanger

帽子

hat

ネクタイ

tie

ファスナー

zip

ヘルメット

helmet

サスペンダー

braces

制服

school uniform

ユニフォーム

uniform

よだれかけ

bib

おしゃぶり

dummy

おむつ

nappy

オフィス
office

紙
paper

書類キャビネット
filing cabinet

プリンター
printer

サーバ
server

モニター
monitor

マウス
mouse

事務机
desk

フォルダー
folder

キーボード
keyboard

ごみ箱
waste-paper basket

コンピューター
computer

椅子
chair

コーヒーマグ

coffee mug

計算機

calculator

インターネット

internet

ラップトップ

laptop

手紙

letter

メッセージ

message

携帯電話

mobile

ネットワーク

network

コピー機

photocopier

ソフトウェア

software

電話

telephone

コンセント

plug socket

ファックス

fax machine

フォーム

form

書類

document

買う

buy

支払う

pay

取引する

trade

お金

money

ドル

dollar

ユーロ

euro

円

yen

ルーブル

rouble

スイスフラン

Swiss franc

人民元

renminbi yuan

ルピー

rupee

キャッシュポイント

cashpoint

両替所

bureau de change

金

gold

銀

silver

油

oil

エネルギー

energy

価格

price

契約

contract

税金

tax

株

stock

働く

work

従業員

employee

雇用主

employer

工場

factory

ショップ

shop

警察官
police officer

消防士
fireman

コック
cook

医師
doctor

パイロット
pilot

庭師

gardener

大工

carpenter

お針子

seamstress

裁判官

judge

化学者

chemist

俳優

actor

バスの運転手

bus driver

タクシー運転手

taxi driver

漁師

fisherman

掃除婦

cleaning lady

屋根ふき職人

roofer

ウェイター

waiter

ハンター

hunter

塗装工

painter

パン屋

baker

電気工

electrician

建設作業員

builder

エンジニア

engineer

肉屋

butcher

配管工

plumber

郵便配達人

postman

軍人
soldier

建築家
architect

レジ係
cashier

花屋
florist

美容師
hairdresser

車掌
conductor

機械工
mechanic

キャプテン
captain

歯科医
dentist

科学者
scientist

ラビ
rabbi

イスラム導師
imam

修道士
monk

牧師
clergyman

道具
tools

ハンマー
hammer

くぎ抜き
pliers

ドライバー
screwdriver

スパナ
spanner

懐中電灯
torch

掘削機

digger

道具箱

toolbox

はしご

ladder

のこぎり

saw

釘

nails

ドリル

drill

修理する

repair

シャベル

shovel

クソ！

Damn!

ちりとり

dustpan

ペンキ缶

paint pot

ネジ

screws

楽器
musical instruments

スピーカー
loudspeaker

打楽器
drum kit

ギター
guitar

コントラバス
double bass

トランペット
trumpet

ピアノ

piano

バイオリン

violin

バス

bass

ティンパニ

timpani

ドラム

drums

キーボード

keyboard

サックス

saxophone

フルート

flute

マイクロフォン

microphone

虎
tiger

入口
▶ entrance

▶ おり
cage

シマウマ
zebra

飼料
animal feed

パンダ
panda

動物

animals

象

elephant

カンガルー

kangaroo

サイ

rhino

ゴリラ

gorilla

熊

bear

ラクダ

camel

ダチョウ

ostrich

ライオン

lion

猿

monkey

フラミンゴ

flamingo

オウム

parrot

白クマ

polar bear

ペンギン

penguin

サメ

shark

クジャク

peacock

蛇

snake

ワニ

crocodile

飼育係

zookeeper

アザラシ

seal

ジャガー

jaguar

ポニー

pony

ヒョウ

leopard

カバ

hippo

キリン

giraffe

鷲

eagle

雄豚

boar

魚

fish

亀

turtle

セイウチ

walrus

狐

fox

ガゼル

gazelle

アメフト
American football

サイクリング
cycling

テニス
tennis

バスケットボール
basketball

水泳
swimming

ボクシング
boxing

アイスホッケー
ice hockey

サッカー
football

バドミントン
badminton

陸上競技
athletics

ハンドボール
handball

スキー
skiing

ポロ
polo

跳ぶ
jump

笑う
laugh

抱きしめる
hug

歩く
walk

歌う
sing

祈る
pray

キス
kiss

夢見る
dream

書く
write

描く
draw

示す
show

押す
push

与える
give

取る
take

持っている
have

する
do

ある
be

立つ
stand

走る
run

引く
pull

投げる
throw

落ちる
fall

横たわっている
lie

待つ
wait

運ぶ
carry

座る
sit

着る
get dressed

眠る
sleep

目が覚める
wake up

見る

look at

泣く

cry

なでる

stroke

櫛ですく

comb

話す

talk

理解する

understand

質問する

ask

聞く

listen

飲む

drink

食べる

eat

片づける

tidy up

愛する

love

料理する

cook

運転する

drive

飛ぶ

fly

ヨットに乗る

sail

計算する

calculate

読む

read

学ぶ

learn

働く

work

結婚する

marry

縫う

sew

歯を磨く

brush teeth

殺す

kill

喫煙する

smoke

送る

send

祖母
grandmother

祖父
grandfather

父
father

母
mother

赤ん坊
baby

娘
daughter

息子
son

お客様
guest

アウント
おば

aunt

おじ

uncle

兄弟
brother

姉妹
sister

ひたい
forehead

目
eye

肩
shoulder

指
finger

顔
face

あご
chin

手
hand

胸
breast

脚
leg

腕
arm

赤ん坊

baby

男性

man

女性

woman

少女

girl

少年

boy

頭

head

背中

back

腹

belly

へそ

belly button

足指

toe

かかと

heel

骨

bone

腰

hip

ひざ

knee

ひじ

elbow

鼻

nose

尻

bottom

皮膚

skin

頬

cheek

耳

ear

唇

lip

体 - body

口
mouth

歯
tooth

舌
tongue

脳
brain

心臓
heart

筋肉
muscle

肺
lung

肝臓
liver

胃
stomach

腎臓
kidneys

セックス
sex

コンドーム
condom

卵細胞
ovum

精液
semen

妊娠
pregnancy

月経

menstruation

膣

vagina

ペニス

penis

眉

eyebrow

髪

hair

首

neck

病院
hospital

救急車
ambulance

車椅子
wheelchair

骨折
fracture

医師
doctor

救急治療室
emergency room

看護師
nurse

救急
emergency

失神
unconscious

痛み
pain

けが

injury

出血

bleeding

心臓発作

heart attack

脳卒中

stroke

アレルギー

allergy

咳

cough

熱

fever

インフルエンザ

flu

下痢

diarrhoea

頭痛

headache

癌

cancer

糖尿病

diabetes

外科医

surgeon

外科用メス

scalpel

手術

operation

CT

CT

レントゲン

x-ray

超音波

ultrasound

マスク

face mask

病気

disease

待合室

waiting room

松葉づえ

crutch

ばんそうこう

plaster

包帯

bandage

注射

injection

聴診器

stethoscope

担架

stretcher

体温計

clinical thermometer

出産

birth

肥満

overweight

補聴器

hearing aid

消毒剤

disinfectant

感染

infection

ウイルス

virus

HIV / エイズ

HIV / AIDS

内服薬

medicine

予防接種

vaccination

錠剤

tablets

ピル

pill

緊急電話

emergency call

血圧計

blood pressure monitor

病気の ／ 健康な

ill / healthy

助けて！

Help!

アラーム

alarm

暴行

assault

攻撃

attack

危険

danger

非常口

emergency exit

火事だ！

Fire!

消火器

fire extinguisher

事故

accident

救急箱

first-aid kit

SOS

SOS

警察

police

ヨーロッパ

Europe

北米

North America

南米

South America

アフリカ

Africa

アジア

Asia

オーストラリア

Australia

大西洋

Atlantic

太平洋

Pacific

インド洋

Indian Ocean

南極海

Antarctic Ocean

北極海

Arctic Ocean

北極

North Pole

南極

South Pole

南極大陸

Antarctica

地球

Earth

陸

land

海

sea

島

island

国家

nation

国家

state

文字盤

clock face

短針

hour hand

長針

minute hand

秒針

second hand

何時ですか？

What time is it?

日

day

時間

time

現在

now

デジタル時計

digital watch

分

minute

時間

hour

週

week

月曜 Monday	水曜 Wednesday	金曜 Friday
火曜 Tuesday	土曜 Saturday	日曜 Sunday
木曜 Thursday		

昨日

yesterday

今日

today

明日

tomorrow

朝

morning

昼

noon

夜

evening

営業日

business days

週末

weekend

雨
rain

虹
rainbow

風
wind

雪
snow

春
spring

秋
autumn

夏
summer

冬
winter

天気予報

weather forecast

温度計

thermometer

日差し

sunshine

雲

cloud

霧

fog

湿度

humidity

雷

lightning

雷

thunder

嵐

storm

ひょう

hail

季節風

monsoon

洪水

flood

氷

ice

1月

January

2月

February

3月

March

4月

April

5月

May

6月

June

7月

July

8月

August

9月
....
September

10月
....
October

11月
....
November

12月
....
December

形

shapes

円
....
circle

正方形
....
square

長方形
....
rectangle

三角
....
triangle

球
....
sphere

立方体
....
cube

色

colours

白
white

黄
yellow

オレンジ
orange

ピンク
pink

赤
red

紫
purple

青
blue

緑
green

茶
brown

灰色
grey

黒
black

多い / 少ない
a lot / a little

怒っている /
落ち着いている
angry / calm

美しい / 醜い
beautiful / ugly

初め / 終わり
beginning / end

大きい / 小さい
big / small

明るい / 暗い
bright / dark

兄弟 / 姉妹
brother / sister

清潔な / 汚い
clean / dirty

完全な / 不完全な
complete / incomplete

日中 / 夜
day / night

死んだ / 生きている
dead / alive

幅広い / 狭い
wide / narrow

食べられる /
食べられない
edible / inedible

悪意のある / 親切な
evil / kind

興奮している /
退屈じでいる
excited / bored

太った / 痩せた
fat / thin

最初に / 最後に
first / last

友人 / 敵
friend / enemy

いっぱいの / 空の
full / empty

硬い / 柔らかい
hard / soft

重い / 軽い
heavy / light

空腹 / 喉の渇き
hunger / thirst

病気の / 健康な
ill / healthy

違法な / 合法な
illegal / legal

賢い / 愚かな
intelligent / stupid

左に / 右に
left / right

近い / 遠い
near / far

新しい ／ 中古の

new / used

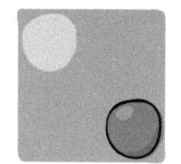

何もない ／ 何かある

nothing / something

老いた ／ 若い

old / young

オン ／ オフ

on / off

開いている ／
閉まっている
open / closed

静かな ／ うるさい

quiet / loud

裕福な ／ 貧乏な

rich / poor

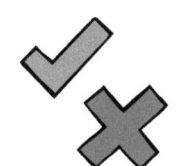

正しい ／ 間違っている

right / wrong

粗い ／ なめらか

rough / smooth

悲しい ／ 幸せな

sad / happy

短い ／ 長い

short / long

ゆっくり ／ 速い

slow / fast

濡れた ／ 乾いた

wet / dry

温かい ／ 冷たい

warm / cool

戦争 ／ 平和

war / peace

反対 - opposites

0

ゼロ
zero

1

1
one

2

2
two

3

3
three

4

4
four

5

5
five

6

6
six

7

7
seven

8

8
eight

9

9
nine

10

10
ten

11

11
eleven

12

12

twelve

13

13

thirteen

14

14

fourteen

15

15

fifteen

16

16

sixteen

17

17

seventeen

18

18

eighteen

19

19

nineteen

20

20

twenty

100

100

hundred

1.000

1000

thousand

1.000.000

100万

million

英語

English

アメリカ英語

American English

中国標準語

Chinese Mandarin

ヒンディー語

Hindi

スペイン語

Spanish

フランス語

French

アラビア語

Arabic

ロシア語

Russian

ポルトガル語

Portuguese

ベンガル語

Bengali

ドイツ語

German

日本語

Japanese

私

I

あなた

you

彼 / 彼女 / それ

he / she / it

私たち

we

あなたたち

you

彼ら

they

誰？

who?

何？

what?

どうやって？

how?

どこ？

where?

いつ？

when?

名前

name

後ろ

behind

中

in

前

in front of

上

over

上

on

下

under

横

beside

間

between

場所

place